THE CASE FOR A
Creator

—

STUDY GUIDE
Revised Edition

Resources by Lee Strobel

The Case for Christ
The Case for Christ audio
The Case for Christ Student Edition (with Jane Vogel)
The Case for Christ curriculum (with Garry Poole)
The Case for Christmas
The Case for Christmas audio
The Case for a Creator
The Case for a Creator audio
The Case for Creator Student Edition (with Jane Vogel)
The Case for a Creator curriculum (with Garry Poole)
The Case for Easter
The Case for Faith
The Case for Faith audio
The Case for Faith Student Edition (with Jane Vogel)
The Case for Faith curriculum (with Garry Poole)
The Case for the Real Jesus
The Case for the Real Jesus audio
Faith Under Fire curriculum
God's Outrageous Claims
Inside the Mind of Unchurched Harry and Mary
Off My Case for Kids
Surviving a Spiritual Mismatch in Marriage (with Leslie Strobel)
Surviving a Spiritual Mismatch in Marriage audio
What Jesus Would Say

Other Resources by Garry Poole

The Complete Book of Questions
Seeker Small Groups

In the Tough Questions Series:

Don't All Religions Lead to God?
How Could God Allow Suffering and Evil?
How Does Anyone Know God Exists?
Why Become a Christian?
Tough Questions Leader's Guide (with Judson Poling)

THE CASE FOR A
Creator
—

*Investigating the Scientific Evidence
That Points toward God*

LEE
STROBEL

NEW YORK TIMES BESTSELLING AUTHOR

AND GARRY POOLE

Revised Edition

ZONDERVAN®
.com

WILLOW
Willow Creek Resources

ZONDERVAN

The Case for a Creator Study Guide Revised Edition
Copyright © 2008, 2013 by Lee Strobel and Garry Poole

This title is also available as a Zondervan ebook. Visit www.zondervan.com/ebooks.

Requests for information should be addressed to:

Zondervan, *Grand Rapids, Michigan 49530*

ISBN 978-0-310-69959-0

Cover design: Faceout Studio
Cover photography: Shutterstock®
Interior design: Beth Shagene

Printed in the United States of America

HB 09.28.2017

Contents

Special thanks to
Laura Allen and Jim Poole
for their outstanding writing and editorial contributions.
Their creative insights and suggestions
took this guide to the next level.

Science and God

I was convinced that science and faith were at odds — and that science definitely had the edge in the credibility department ... And rather than facing an "unyielding despair" that's implicit in a world without God, I reveled in my newly achieved freedom from God's moral strictures. For me, living without God meant living 100 percent for myself. Freed from someday being held accountable for my actions, I felt unleashed to pursue personal happiness and pleasure at all costs ... As a journalist, I was unshackled to compete without always having to abide by those pesky rules of ethics and morality. I would let nothing, and certainly nobody, stand between me and my ambitions.

Lee Strobel, *The Case for a Creator*

Read This!

If possible, read the following book content in preparation for your group meeting: *The Case for a Creator*, chapter 4: Where Science Meets Faith, or *The Case for a Creator Student Edition*, chapter 1: Science vs. God? Otherwise, read it as follow-up.

Watch This!

Video Teaching Segment

Space is provided to take notes on anything that stands out to you.

"Ironically, to say that science is the only begetter of truth is self-contradicting, because that statement in itself cannot be tested by scientific method. It's a self-defeating philosophical assumption."

— Stephen C. Meyer

Discuss This!

1. How much confidence do you put in science as a source of truth? How did you develop the level of trust (or lack thereof) you currently have?

THINK ABOUT THIS!

Some people claim that we live in a technological culture where science trumps all other forms of knowledge. Only science is rational; only science achieves truth. Everything else is mere belief and opinion. If something cannot be qualified or tested by the scientific method, then it cannot be true or rational. Science represents the empirical, the hard facts, and the experimentally proven. Everything else can be dismissed as being mere opinion, superstition — and mindless faith.

2. To what degree do you believe that only science is rational and everything else is mere opinion, superstition, or mindless faith?

> *"It was my science that drove me to the conclusion that the world was much more complicated than can be explained by science."*
> — Cosmologist Allan Sandage

3. Has scientific progress made God unnecessary? Why or why not?

THINK ABOUT THIS!

"The whole point of faith is to believe regardless of the evidence, which is the very antithesis of science."

Michael Shermer, publisher, *Skeptic* magazine

"Religion is something left over from the infancy of our intelligence; it will fade away as we adopt reason and science as our guidelines."

Atheistic philosopher Bertrand Russell

"Proof is only applicable to very rarefied areas of philosophy and mathematics … For the most part we are driven to acting on good evidence, without the luxury of proof. There is good evidence of the link between cause and effect. There is good evidence that the sun will rise tomorrow. There is good reason to believe that I am the same man as I was ten years ago. There is good reason to believe my mother loves me and is not just fattening me up for the moment when she will pop arsenic into my tea. And there is good reason to believe in God. Very good reason. Not conclusive proof, but very good reason just the same … I believe it is much harder to reject the existence of a supreme being than accept it."

Michael Green, *Faith for the Non-Religious*

"You can't absolutely prove — or disprove — the existence of God."

Science philosopher Stephen C. Meyer

4. To what extent do you think it is possible to prove — or disprove — the existence of God? In terms of your own investigation, what level of evidence (or proof) would be sufficient for you to believe or disbelieve the existence of God? How likely is it that there would ever be enough evidence to eliminate your doubts (one way or the other)? What are the implications of your answers?

> *"For those who believe in God,*
> *no explanation is necessary.*
> *For those who do not,*
> *no explanation is possible."*
> — Opening lines of the film
> *The Song of Bernadette*

5. If science is, in fact, the search for truth, should scientists be free to consider the possibility of the supernatural if the evidence of cosmology, physics, and biochemistry points in that direction? Why or why not?

> *"I believe that the testimony of science*
> *supports theism. While there will always*
> *be points of tension or unresolved conflict,*
> *the major developments in science in the*
> *past five decades have been running in a*
> *strongly theistic direction. Science,*
> *done right, points toward God."*
> — Stephen C. Meyer

6. Is it possible to believe in science and also believe in God? Can faith in God ever be rational? Why or why not?

"I didn't see any God out there."
— Yuri Gagarin, Soviet cosmonaut,
after orbiting Earth

THINK ABOUT THIS!

"You will understand that my atheism was inevitably based on what I believed to be the finding of the sciences, and those findings, not being a scientist, I had to take on trust."

C. S. Lewis, *Surprised by Joy*

"I'd have to say that the biggest reason why I don't believe in god is because there is no proof of his existence. Throughout the millions of years that man has been on earth, there has never been any solid evidence that there is a creator. If there is a god, wouldn't he want as many followers as possible? Why leave any doubt? Why not come to earth and tell everyone he exists? Or, better yet, make it so that everyone knows he is there."

Norm, in an online discussion

7. Which of the following "isms" most accurately reflects your current position? What influences or factors prompted you to arrive at this perspective? How long have you held this position?

- **Agnosticism:** the belief that knowledge of the existence or nonexistence of God is impossible

- **Atheism:** the disbelief in the existence of God

- **Deism:** the belief in a supreme being who remains unknowable and untouchable and permits the universe to run itself according to natural laws

- **Fideism:** the belief that matters of religion are not supported by evidence or reason and all that is required is faith

- **Pantheism:** the belief that God and the universe are one

- **Polytheism:** the belief in many gods

- **Theism:** the belief in the existence of God

"All I have seen teaches me to trust the Creator for all I have not seen."
— Ralph Waldo Emerson

THINK ABOUT THIS!

"Some claim science and faith are fundamentally at odds. Others have said science and faith represent two separate and distinct realms that don't and can't interact with each other. However, I personally take a third approach, which is that scientific evidence actually supports theistic belief. In fact, across a wide range of sciences, evidence has come to light in the last fifty years which, taken together, provides a robust case for theism. Only theism can provide an intellectually satisfying causal explanation for all of this evidence."

Stephen C. Meyer

8. Are science and faith at odds? Can science and faith *ever* be compatible? Must a science-minded person reject religious beliefs? Explain your answers.

"God gave us ... two powerful and well-matched abilities: to prove things we find hard to believe and to believe in things we find hard to prove."
— Michael Guillen, *Can a Smart Person Believe in God?*

THINK ABOUT THIS!

"I believe only and alone in the service of Jesus Christ. In him is all refuge and solace."

Johannes Kepler, who discovered the laws
of planetary motion and elliptical orbits

"At the center of every human being is a God-shaped vacuum which can only be filled by Jesus Christ."

Blaise Pascal, father of the mathematical theory
of probability and combinational analysis

"If we need an atheist for a debate, I'd go to the philosophy department — the physics department isn't much use."

Charles Coulson, an architect of molecular orbital theory

"I think of God as the greatest scientist. We human scientists have an opportunity to understand the elegance and wisdom of God's creation in a way that is truly exhilarating. When a scientist discovers something that no human knew before, but God did — that is both an occasion for scientific excitement and, for a believer, also an occasion for worship."

Francis Collins, director of the Human Genome Project,
which first mapped all the genes of human beings

9. To what extent can we separate ourselves from our own biases? How much do our religious or atheistic preconceived notions and worldview taint the conclusions we draw? How might *your* current view of God — positive or negative — affect the way you assess the scientific evidence for his existence?

THINK ABOUT THIS!

"Question boldly even the existence of God."

Thomas Jefferson

"Do not be afraid to be free thinkers. If you think strongly enough, you will be forced by science to the belief in God."

William Thompson, physical scientist and teacher

"Let's have a new period in the history of science where we have methodological rules that actually foster the unfettered seeking of truth. Scientists should be allowed to follow the evidence wherever it leads — even if it leads to a conclusion that makes some people uncomfortable."

Stephen C. Meyer

OPTIONAL DISCUSSION QUESTIONS
for Those Investigating Christianity

• Is there any limit to what man can discover scientifically? If so, what are the limits of science? If not, what are the possibilities?

• Which of the following statements do you think are true in spite of the fact that they cannot be tested or validated scientifically? What are some other examples of traits, values, or truths that exist but cannot be explained by science alone?

  – Humans have the capacity to love.

  – Humans have the capacity to self-reflect.

  – Humans have consciences.

  – Humans are creative creatures.

  – It is better to love than to hate.

  – It is wrong to murder an innocent person.

• Because scientific theories can change over time, how reliable is what we learn from science today? To what extent do you think future scientific discoveries will disprove current scientific understanding?

• Do most people you know believe that Christianity and evolution are either/or concepts or both/and ideas? Do you agree with Lee's conclusion that if life emerged out of naturalistic circumstances, God is out of a job?

• Physicist John Polkinghorne asserts that science and religion are friends, not foes, united by the common quest for knowledge. Do you agree with this assertion? Are you open to the possibility? Why or why not?

Between Sessions

Personal Reflection

"For I know the plans I have for you," declares the LORD, "plans to prosper you and not to harm you, plans to give you hope and a future. Then you will call on me and come and pray to me, and I will listen to you. You will seek me and find me when you seek me with all your heart."

(Jeremiah 29:11–13)

1. Do you gravitate toward or away from scientific inquiry? What about religious inquiry? How curious are you about God?

2. Carefully meditate on the above verses from Jeremiah and just imagine these are God's words to you personally. What is your response? Are you skeptical? Bemused? Cynical? Or do you feel a spark of hope that this concept might be real? Try this exercise: Suspend your disbelief, just for a moment, and consider the possibility that God is real, that he cares about you, and that he invites you to seek and find him. How does this possibility impact you?

3. Now reread the promise made to you in the last sentence of the Jeremiah passage. What if God is real and keeps all his promises? Notice, though, that the promise is conditional—you must do your part. How willing are you to seek truth sincerely with your whole heart and to follow the evidence wherever it leads? What might hold you back from such an open-minded search?

4. Jesus once had a conversation with one of his followers who admitted to him, "Lord, I believe, now help me with my unbelief!" Can you relate in any way to this man's honest and heartfelt plea? How surprising is it to you to discover that the Bible identifies many people who faced doubts about God, and yet he answered them? You can rest assured that God welcomes your objections, questions, and doubts—and that he even invites you to come to him with your unbelief!

Personal Reading

Please read the following book content in preparation for session two:

The Case for a Creator, chapter 2: The Images of Evolution

The Case for a Creator, chapter 3: Doubts about Darwinism

Or, *The Case for a Creator Student Edition*, chapter 3: Exploring Evolution

Doubts about Darwinism

It was no accident that my admiration for scientific thinking was developing at the same time that my confidence in God was waning. In Sunday school and confirmation classes during my junior high school years, my "why" questions weren't always welcomed. So the seeds of my atheism were sown as a youngster when religious authorities seemed unwilling or unable to help me get answers to my questions about God. My disbelief flowered after discovering that Darwinism displaces the need for a deity. And my atheism came to full bloom when I studied Jesus in college and was told that no science-minded person could possibly believe what the New Testament says about him.

Lee Strobel, *The Case for a Creator*

Watch This!

Video Teaching Segment

Space is provided to take notes on anything that stands out to you.

"*If you meet somebody who claims not to believe in evolution, that person is ignorant, stupid, or insane, (or wicked, but I'd rather not consider that).*"

— Atheist and evolutionary
biologist Richard Dawkins

Discuss This!

1. What's your immediate reaction to the illustration above? What thoughts or emotions does this picture elicit in you?

2. Describe Darwinian evolution as you currently understand it. Is it a theory or a fact? How has Darwinism evolved over time? What do you think people usually mean by the term "evolution"? What about the phrase "natural selection"?

THE STANLEY MILLER EXPERIMENT

The Old Story of Science

Miller used the hydrogen-rich mixture of methane, ammonia, and water vapor to demonstrate how the early atmosphere created amino acids, the building blocks of life.

The New Story of Science

Scientists today know that these were not the elements of the primitive atmosphere on earth. Miller's experiment has been repeated many times using the correct atmospheric components: carbon dioxide, nitrogen, water vapor, and very little hydrogen. The results are always the same: this mixture produces at best formaldehyde, but not amino acids, the building blocks of life.

THINK ABOUT THIS!

"Even if scientists could somehow manage to produce amino acids from the correct mixture of elements of the early atmosphere, how far would they be from creating a living cell? You would have to get the right number of the right kinds of amino acids to link up to create a protein molecule — and that would still be a long way from a living cell. Then you'd need dozens of protein molecules, again in the right sequence, to create a living cell. The odds against this are astonishing. The gap between nonliving chemicals and even the most primitive living organisms is absolutely tremendous. The problem of assembling the right parts in the right way at the right time and at the right place, while keeping out the wrong material, is simply insurmountable."

Biologist Jonathan Wells

3. Read the "Stanley Miller Experiment" on the previous page and the "Think About This!" box above regarding the low probability of amino acids ever producing life. Do you agree or disagree with this reasoning? Explain your answer.

4. What's the theory behind Darwin's tree of life? (See the "Darwin's 'Tree of Life'" box on the next page.) Does it make sense to you? Why or why not? What questions does it raise for you?

"If you consider all the evidence, Darwin's tree is false as a description of the history of life. It's not even a good hypothesis at this point."
— Jonathan Wells

DARWIN'S "TREE OF LIFE"

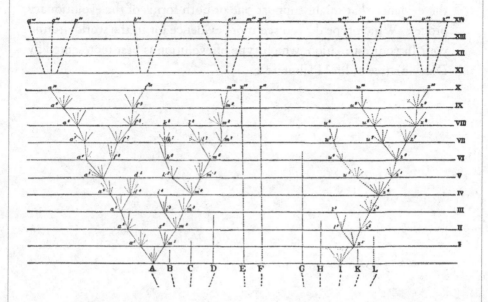

The Old Story of Science

All living creatures have a common ancestor. Starting with an ancient ancestor at the bottom, the tree blossoms upward into limbs, branches, and twigs that represent life evolving with increasing diversity and complexity. If a population were exposed to one set of conditions, and another part of the population experienced other conditions, then natural selection would modify the two populations in different ways. Over time, one species could produce several varieties, and if these varieties continued to diverge, they would eventually, over an enormous amount of time, become separate species. This theory predicts a long history of gradual divergence from a common ancestor, with differences slowly becoming bigger and bigger until we get the major differences we have now.

The New Story of Science

The fossil evidence to this day shows the opposite effect: a rapid appearance of phylum-level differences in what's called the Cambrian explosion. There is evidence of microevolution (changes within a species), but there are no conclusive examples of macroevolution (transitional forms between major kinds of creatures). In short, the Cambrian explosion has uprooted Darwin's tree.

5. According to the "Fast Fact" definitions below, what is the main difference between microevolution and macroevolution? Give examples of the evidence that might support one or both forms of the evolutionary process. Which type do you see more evidence for in the world around you? In your estimation, which type of evolution is best represented by Darwin's tree of life? Elaborate.

FAST FACT

Microevolution: *Comparatively minor, gradual evolutionary change involving the accumulation of variations within a species*

Macroevolution: *Gradual evolution that results in relatively large and complex changes (as in species formation)*

6. Read the "Think About This!" box on the next page. What do you think Darwin would say today about the fact that the fossil record has never supported his theory of a gradual evolutionary process?

THINK ABOUT THIS!

"The most obvious and gravest objection which can be urged against my theory [is the fossil record]. Why, if species have descended from other species by insensibly fine gradations, do we not everywhere see innumerable transitional forms?"

Charles Darwin, *The Origin of Species*

"Who knows how natural history might be rewritten next week by a discovery that will be made in a fossil dig somewhere? Is it possible that someone will discover a fossil bed somewhere that will suddenly fill in the gaps? Not likely. It hasn't happened after all this time, and millions of fossils have already been dug up. There are certainly enough good sedimentary rocks from before the Cambrian era to have preserved ancestors if there were any. The Cambrian explosion is too big to be masked by flaws in the fossil record."

Jonathan Wells

"The universal experience of paleontology is that while the rocks have continually yielded new and exciting and even bizarre forms of life ... what they have never yielded is any of Darwin's myriads of transitional forms. Despite the tremendous increase in geological activity in every corner of the globe and despite the discovery of many strange and hitherto unknown forms, the infinitude of connecting links has still not been discovered and the fossil record is about as discontinuous as it was when Darwin was writing Origin. *The intermediates have remained as elusive as ever and their absence remains, a century later, one of the most striking characteristics of the fossil record."*

Molecular geneticist Michael Denton, *Evolution: A Theory in Crisis*

7. Read the quotes in the "Think About This!" box that follows. To what extent do you agree with Wells's assessment? In what ways do you disagree? What is your reaction to the increasing number of scientists who have moved away from Darwinian evolution toward Intelligent Design?

THINK ABOUT THIS!

"I believe science is strongly pointing toward design. To me, as a scientist, the development of an embryo cries out, 'Design!' The Cambrian explosion — the sudden appearance of complex life, with no evidence of ancestors — is more consistent with design than evolution ... The origin of life certainly cries out for a designer. None of these things make as much sense from a Darwinian perspective as they do from a design perspective. When you analyze all the most current affirmative evidence from cosmology, physics, astronomy, biology, and so forth — well, I think you'll discover that the positive case for an intelligent designer becomes absolutely compelling.

"My conclusion is that the case for Darwinian evolution is bankrupt. The evidence for Darwinism is not only grossly inadequate, it's systematically distorted.

I'm convinced that sometime in the not-too-distant future — I don't know, maybe twenty or thirty years from now — people will look back in amazement and say, 'How could anyone have believed this?' Darwinism is merely materialistic philosophy masquerading as science, and people are recognizing it for what it is."

Jonathan Wells

"We are skeptical of claims for the ability of random mutation and natural selection to account for the complexity of life … Careful examination of the evidence for Darwinian theory should be encouraged."

"A Scientific Dissent from Darwinism," signed by more than 600 scientists with doctorates from a variety of institutions

"The claim that all skeptics about Darwinian orthodoxy are Christian fundamentalists stands refuted by me. I am neither a Christian nor a fundamentalist, but lots and lots of people are skeptical in the scientific community."

David Berlinski, PhD, Princeton University

"Scientists who utterly reject evolution may be one of our fastest-growing controversial minorities … Many of the scientists supporting this position hold impressive credentials in science."

Larry Hatfield in *Science Digest*

"There is no encompassing theory of human evolution. Alas, there never really has been."

Anthropologist F. Clark Howell

"The controversy in modern times is not between science and religion, it's between two different interpretations of the same scientific evidence. It's not science vs. religion, it's science vs. science."

Stephen C. Meyer, PhD, History and Philosophy of Science, Cambridge University

OPTIONAL DISCUSSION QUESTIONS
for Those Investigating Christianity

- To what extent do you trust what you were taught in school about evolution?

- Stephen C. Meyer, among others, believes it's contradictory to say that God guides an inherently unguided natural process or that God designed a natural mechanism as a substitute for his design. Do you think it is possible to believe in Darwinian evolution and still believe in the existence of God, or are evolution and creationism mutually exclusive? In other words, does Darwinism really explain away the need for a Creator? Explain your answer.

- Which of the following quotes do you agree with most? Least? Why?

  "I think people who believe that life emerged naturalistically need to have a great deal more faith than people who reasonably infer that there's an Intelligent Designer."

  —Walter Bradley, *The Mystery of Life's Origin*

  "The more you understand the significance of evolution, the more you are pushed away from an agnostic position and towards atheism."

  —Oxford evolutionist Richard Dawkins

  "As for me, I finally came to the point where I realized that I just didn't have enough faith to maintain my belief in Darwinism. The evidence in my estimation was simply unable to support its grandest and most sweeping claims."

  —Lee Strobel

- Speculate on some of the possible explanations for the zeal surrounding the scientifically incorrect conclusions regarding the alleged "transitional" fossils. In your opinion, why do scientists cling to outdated information related to evolution?

Between Sessions

Personal Reflection

And God said, "Let the water teem with living creatures, and let birds fly above the earth across the vault of the sky." So God created the great creatures of the sea and every living with which the water teems and that moves about in it, according to their kinds, and every winged bird according to its kind. And God saw that it was good. God blessed them and said, "Be fruitful and increase in number and fill the water in the seas, and let the birds increase on the earth." ... And God said, "Let the land produce living creatures according to their kinds: the livestock, the creatures that move along the ground, and the wild animals, each according to its kind." And it was so. God made the wild animals according to their kinds, the livestock according to their kinds, and all the creatures that move along the ground according to their kinds. And God saw that it was good.

(Genesis 1:20–22, 24–25)

1. Growing up, how did what you learned about evolution affect your spiritual outlook or influence your beliefs about God? To what degree do you consider yourself to be open-minded regarding the issue of evolution? How willing are you to be challenged by new discoveries that may differ from what you've learned in the past?

2. Think about an occasion when you had a significant understanding or belief exposed as inaccurate. How long had you held your erroneous view before it was somehow corrected? How did the process of discovery make you feel at the time? Resistant, embarrassed, angry? Or as a truth-seeker, were you grateful to find out the truth of the matter?

3. To what extent do you feel that doubts you may have had regarding God's existence were unacceptable and unwelcome? What were the circumstances or situations that fostered such attitudes in others around you? How might those past experiences impact the intensity of your spiritual search now?

4. According to Genesis 1:20–22, 24–25 quoted at the beginning of the "Personal Reflection," what exactly does the Bible claim to be true about the origin of the species? What does it say about each species' offspring? Do the creatures appear suddenly, as the Cambrian explosion and the fossil record seem to indicate, or do they form gradually over time, as Darwinian macroevolutionists hold? Which scientific evidence or theory aligns most closely with what the Bible teaches?

5. The Bible describes the Creator as a "God of knowledge" and says that his wisdom far surpasses that of any mere human. Are you surprised to learn that this same God promises to give wisdom to anyone who genuinely asks for it, including *you*? Why not go to God now in prayer and ask for wisdom regarding the origin—and perhaps even the meaning—of life?

Personal Reading

Please read the following book content in preparation for session three:

> *The Case for a Creator*, chapter 5: The Evidence of Cosmology
>
> Or, *The Case for a Creator Student Edition*, chapter 2: Beginning
>   with a Bang

The Evidence of Cosmology

My eyes scanned the magazines at the newsstand near my home. A beautiful woman graced Glamour. Sleek, high-performance cars streaked across the front of Motor Trend. And there on the cover of Discover magazine, sitting by itself, unadorned, floating in a sea of pure white background, was a simple red sphere. It was smaller than a tennis ball, tinier than a Titleist — just three quarters of an inch in diameter, not too much bigger than a marble. As staggering as it seemed, it represented the actual size of the entire universe when it was just an infinitesimal fraction of one second old. The headline cried out: Where Did Everything Come From?

Lee Strobel, *The Case for a Creator*

Watch This!

Video Teaching Segment

Space is provided to take notes on anything that stands out to you.

"It seems impossible that you could get
something from nothing, but the fact that
once there was nothing and now there is
a universe is evident proof that you can."
— Bill Bryson, *A Short History
of Nearly Everything*

Discuss This!

1. Why do you think the issue about how the universe began is controversial for many people?

FAST FACT

Cosmologist: *A scientist who studies the origin of the universe*

---

2. Do you believe the universe has always existed in an eternal unchanging state? Or do you think the universe had an absolute beginning somewhere in the finite past? Give reasons for your opinion. Which position were you taught growing up?

3. The assumption ever since the ancient Greeks has been that the material world is eternal. Christians have denied this on the basis of biblical revelation, but secular science always assumed the universe's eternality. What do you think was the rationale behind why scientists once believed the universe always existed?

"It's important to understand how reversed the situation is from a hundred years ago. Back then, Christians had to maintain by faith in the Bible that despite all appearances to the contrary, the universe was not eternal but was created out of nothing a finite time ago. Now the situation is exactly the opposite."
— William Lane Craig

4. Do you think it is reasonable to conclude that if the universe is, in fact, continually expanding, then at earlier points in its history it must have been smaller and denser, to such an extent that the entire known universe began from a single point of infinite density called a "singularity"? Can you think of another viable theory behind the continual expansion of the universe? Give reasons for your answer.

"The most reasonable belief is that we came from nothing, by nothing, and for nothing."
— Atheist Quentin Smith

5. According to Stephen Hawking, "Almost everyone now believes that the universe, and time itself, had a beginning at the Big Bang." When did you first become familiar with the Big Bang theory? What was your initial opinion of the theory at that time? What is your opinion now?

"Set aside the many competing explanations of the Big Bang; something made an entire cosmos out of nothing. It is this realization — that something transcendent started it all — which has hard-science types … using terms like 'miracle.'"
— Journalist Gregg Easterbrook

THINK ABOUT THIS!

Empirical Data for the Big Bang

"In the 1920s, the Russian mathematician Alexander Friedman and the Belgium astronomer George Lemaître were able to develop models based on Einstein's theory. They predicted the universe was expanding. Of course, this meant that if you went backward in time, the universe would go back to a single origin before which it didn't exist. Astronomer Fred Hoyle derisively called this the Big Bang — and the name stuck!

"In 1929, the American astronomer Edwin Hubble discovered that the light coming to us from distant galaxies appears to be redder than it should be, and that this is a universal feature of galaxies in all parts of the sky. Hubble explained this red shift as being due to the fact that the galaxies are moving away from us. He concluded that the universe is literally flying apart at enormous velocities.

cont.

"In the 1940s, George Gamow predicted that if the Big Bang really happened, then the background temperature of the universe should be just a few degrees above absolute zero ... Sure enough, in 1965, two scientists accidentally discovered the universe's background radiation — and it was only about 3.7 degrees above absolute zero.

"Predictions about the Big Bang have been consistently verified by scientific data. Moreover, they have been corroborated by the failure of every attempt to falsify them by alternative models. Unquestionably, the Big Bang model has impressive scientific credentials."

William Lane Craig

6. The *kalam* cosmological argument provides three simple steps to a line of reasoning for God's existence: (1) whatever begins to exist has a cause; (2) the universe began to exist; (3) therefore, the universe has a cause. Do you agree with the deductive reasoning behind the *kalam* argument? Why or why not? If not, where do you believe the argument falls apart?

NOTE: In *The Case for a Creator* (pages 108–112), William Lane Craig demonstrates logically from the evidence that the Creator must be an uncaused, beginningless, timeless, spaceless, immaterial, personal being endowed with freedom of will and enormous power — all unmistakable attributes of the divine.

PREMISE #1

Whatever begins to exist has a cause.

"We certainly have empirical evidence for the truth of this premise. This is a principle that is constantly confirmed and never falsified. We never see things coming into being uncaused out of nothing."

William Lane Craig

"I never asserted so absurd a proposition as that anything might arise without a cause."

Renowned skeptic David Hume (1754)

PREMISE #2

The universe began to exist.

"In the beginning there was an explosion. Not an explosion like those familiar on Earth, starting from a definite center and spreading out to engulf more and more of the circumambient air, but an explosion which occurred simultaneously everywhere, filling all space from the beginning with every particle of matter rushing apart from every other particle."

Physicist Steven Weinberg, *The First Three Minutes*

PREMISE #3

Therefore, the universe has a cause.

"In atheism, the universe just pops into being out of nothing, with absolutely no explanation at all. I think once people understand the concept of absolute nothingness, it's simply obvious to them that if something has a beginning, that it could not have popped into being out of nothing but must have a cause that brings it into existence."

William Lane Craig

7. It is one thing to state that the universe has a cause, and quite another thing to claim that fact leads to theological implications. How big of a leap is it to deduce that since the universe has a cause, that cause must therefore be a divine being? Explain.

"Even atheist Kai Nielsen said, 'Suppose you suddenly hear a loud bang ... and you ask me, "What made that bang?" and I reply, "Nothing, it just happened." You would not accept that.' He's right, of course. And if a cause is needed for a small bang like that, then it's needed for the Big Bang as well."
— William Lane Craig

THINK ABOUT THIS!

"If everything must have a cause, then the First Cause must be caused and therefore: Who made God? To say that this First Cause always existed is to deny the basic assumption of this theory."

David Marshall Brooks, *The Necessity of Atheism*

"I never said everything must have a cause. The premise is that whatever begins to exist must have a cause. In other words, 'being' can't come from 'nonbeing.' Since God never began to exist [that is, he never had a beginning], he doesn't require a cause. He never came into being.... Atheists themselves used to be very comfortable in maintaining that the universe is eternal and uncaused. The problem is that

they can no longer hold that position because of modern evidence that the universe started with the Big Bang. So they can't legitimately object when I make the same claim about God — he is eternal and he is uncaused."

William Lane Craig

8. Atheist George Smith states, "If *everything* must have a cause, how did God become exempt?" How would you respond to Smith's question?

9. Theoretical physicist Stephen Hawking said, "We are such insignificant creatures on a minor planet of a very average star in the outer suburbs of one of a hundred thousand million galaxies. So it is difficult to believe in a God that would care about us or even notice our existence." Do you agree? Why or why not?

OPTIONAL DISCUSSION QUESTIONS
for Those Investigating Christianity

- Does it take more faith to accept that the universe had no cause or to accept that there had to be a First Cause to all that exists?

- What's the difference, if any, between an expanding universe and an evolving universe?

- Do you believe the universe is expanding and will continue to expand indefinitely? Is that compatible with the world around you as you experience it? Why or why not?

- Christians often caution that a skeptic cannot be argued into faith. Yet if someone were sincerely open-minded, could the *kalam* cosmological argument be sufficient to prompt a verdict in favor of a supernatural Creator? Or would it merely become fodder for more and more creative— or, as some might say, desperate—counterarguments and objections?

- Is God dead? Is it possible that a Creator put the universe in motion, but later ceased to exist? How would you formulate a response to this possibility?

- William Lane Craig suggests that God is personal. What does that mean? Define "personal creator." How would this be different from "The Force" of *Star Wars*? What are some of the implications for us if God is personal?

Between Sessions

Personal Reflection

> *In the beginning God created the heavens and the earth. Now the earth was formless and empty, darkness was over the surface of the deep, and the Spirit of God was hovering over the waters. And God said, "Let there be light," and there was light. God saw that the light was good.*

> (Genesis 1:1–4a)

1. Carefully read the Genesis account above, and then compare and contrast this description with what you understand science has discovered regarding the origin of the universe. In what ways does this 3,500-year-old passage align with the Big Bang theory?

2. Think about the universe and how vast, incredible, and awe-inspiring it is. How unbelievable is it to you that the chain of events leading to your life in this very moment—all matter, space, and even time—originated instantaneously out of nothing, in a flash of light and energy?

3. Thousands of years ago, the Hebrews believed everything began with the primordial *fiat lux*—the voice of God commanding light into existence. Do you believe that something as expansive as the universe could have come out of absolutely nothing? How much of a stretch is it for you to consider the possibility that a divine Creator has always existed and caused that moment to occur? To what extent does this claim, regardless of its source, require you to take a leap of faith?

4. The biblical book of Hebrews (11:1 – 3) teaches, "Now faith is confidence in what we hope for and assurance about what we do not see. This is what the ancients were commended for. By faith we understand that the universe was formed at God's command, so that what is seen was not made out of what was visible." Think about some examples of things you are sure of, but you cannot actually see. If faith is being certain of what cannot be seen, what do you currently have faith in?

5. If you'd like, take a few moments to sincerely acknowledge your doubts about the origin of the universe with a simple, honest prayer. If God is real and has the power to create something as spectacular as billions of galaxies, wouldn't he also have the power to help you increase your faith? Why not suspend your disbelief for the moment and give God an opportunity to respond to you?

Personal Reading

Please read the following book content in preparation for session four:

> *The Case for a Creator*, chapter 6: The Evidence of Physics
>
> *The Case for a Creator*, chapter 7: The Evidence of Astronomy
>
> Or, *The Case for a Creator Student Edition*, chapter 4: The Cosmos on a Razor's Edge

The Fine-tuning
of the Universe

It's turning out that the Earth is anything but ordinary, that our sun is far from average, and that even the position of our planet in the galaxy is eerily fortuitous. The idea that the universe is a flourishing hothouse of advanced civilizations is now being undermined by surprising new scientific discoveries and fresh thinking… Whichever way I looked, the inference of design seemed inescapable. If ours is the only universe in existence, which is a logical conclusion based on the evidence, then its highly sophisticated fine-tuning cries out for a designer.

Lee Strobel, *The Case for a Creator*

Watch This!

Video Teaching Segment

Space is provided to take notes on anything that stands out to you.

Discuss This!

1. Read the "Think About This!" box on the next page. Then answer this question: If the universe were put on trial for a charge of having been designed, and the fine-tuning of the cosmological constant and the force of gravity were the only evidence introduced, would you vote "guilty" or "not guilty"? Elaborate.

"It is quite easy to understand why so many scientists have changed their minds in the past thirty years, agreeing that the universe cannot reasonably be explained as a cosmic accident. Evidence for an intelligent designer becomes more compelling the more we understand our carefully crafted habitat."
— Scientist Walter Bradley

THINK ABOUT THIS!

"Imagine a ruler, or one of those old-fashioned linear radio dials, that goes all the way across the universe. It would be broken down into one-inch increments, which means there would be billions upon billions upon billions of inches. The entire dial represents the range of force strengths in nature, with gravity being the weakest force and the strong nuclear force that binds protons and neutrons together in the nuclei being the strongest, a whopping ten thousand billion billion billion billion times stronger than gravity. The range of possible settings for the force of gravity can plausibly be taken to be at least as large as the total range of force strengths. Now, let's imagine that you want to move the dial from where it's currently set. Even if you were to move it by only one inch, the impact on life in the universe would be catastrophic ... Animals anywhere near the size of human beings would be crushed."

Robin Collins

"The cosmological constant (the expansion speed of space in the universe), which is part of Einstein's equation for general relativity, could have had any value, positive or negative. If large and positive, the cosmological constant would act as a repulsive force that increases with distance, a force that would prevent matter from clumping together in the early universe, the process that was the first step in forming galaxies and stars and planets and people. If large and negative, the cosmological constant would act as an attractive force increasing with distance, a force that would almost immediately reverse the expansion of the universe and cause it to recollapse. In fact, astronomical observations show that the cosmological constant is quite small, very much smaller than would have been guessed from first principles."

Nobel Prize – winning physicist Steven Weinberg

2. If a Creator really does exist, would you expect the universe to be deliberate and directed or random and undirected? Elaborate.

THINK ABOUT THIS!

"The fine-tuning of the universe refers to the extraordinary balancing of the fundamental laws and parameters of physics and the initial conditions of the universe. Our minds can't comprehend the precision of some of them. The result is a universe that has just the right conditions to sustain life. The coincidences are simply too amazing to have been the result of happenstance. Over the past thirty years or so, scientists have discovered that just about everything about the basic structure of the universe is balanced on a razor's edge for life to exist."

Robin Collins

There are more than thirty separate parameters that require precise calibration in order to produce a life-sustaining universe, including:

- Gravitational force
- Electromagnetic force
- Strong nuclear force
- Weak nuclear force
- Speed of light
- Planck's constant
- Proton mass
- Electron mass
- Cosmological constant
- Mass density of the universe
- Carlson energy resonance
- Water
- Original phase – space volume
- 26 essential elements required for human life
- Galactic Habitable Zone
- Earth's composition of elements
- A spiral galaxy (and Earth's location in it)
- A circular orbit
- Surrounding planets
- Circumstellar Habitable Zone
- An uncommon sun — yellow dwarf star
- A large moon
- The mass (size) of the earth
- Oxygen-rich atmosphere (20 percent)
- Plate tectonics
- The earth's albedo (reflectivity)

3. Can you think of ways to try to explain away the universe's fine-tuning? How well do those alternative explanations deal with the evidence?

"An honest man, armed with all the knowledge available to us now, could only state that in some sense, the origin of life appears at the moment to be almost a miracle, so many are the conditions which would have had to have been satisfied to get it going."
— Nobel Prize winner Francis Crick

4. Physicist Paul Davies asks, "If the world's finest minds can unravel only with difficulty the deeper workings of nature, how could it be supposed that those workings are merely a mindless accident, a product of blind chance?" How would you respond to his question? Can luck really explain why the Earth enjoys this incredible convergence of extremely unlikely circumstances that have allowed human beings to flourish?

"Uncovering the laws of physics resembles completing a crossword [puzzle] in a number of ways ... In the case of the crossword, it would never occur to us to suppose that the words just happened to fall into a consistent interlocking pattern by accident."
— Paul Davies

5. Astronomer George Greenstein asks, "Is it possible that suddenly, without intending to, we have stumbled upon scientific proof of the existence of a Supreme Being? Was it God who stepped in and so providentially crafted the cosmos for our benefit?" What do you think?

6. In the video segment, Jay Richards states that the "multi-universe" theory is "an interesting idea, but there's really only one problem with it. There's no independent evidence that it's true. Besides, it really just pushes the question back a step because we could still ask who built the generator [that would be needed to produce the multiple universes]." If it could be substantiated that there are multiple universes in existence, does that increase or decrease the likelihood that our finely tuned universe was a product of chance? Why? How would the existence of life elsewhere affect your spiritual views?

THINK ABOUT THIS!

"The 'multiple universe' argument can be summarized this way: 'There could have been millions and millions of different universes, each created with different dial settings of the fundamental ratios and constants, so many in fact that the right set was bound to turn up by sheer chance. We just happen to be the lucky ones.'"

Robert Jastrow, *God and the Astronomers*

cont.

"You would need to make trillions upon trillions upon trillions upon trillions of universes in order to increase the odds that the cosmological constant would come out right at least once, since it's finely tuned to an incomprehensible degree. And that's just one parameter."

Robin Collins

"Regardless of which multiple-universe theory you use, in every case you'd need a 'many-universes generator' — and it would require the right structure, the right mechanism, and the right ingredients to churn out new universes. It's highly unlikely that such a universe-generating system would have all the right components in place by random chance, just like random chance can't account for how a bread-maker produces loaves of edible bread. So if a many-universe-generating system exists, there would still need to be an intelligent designer to make the finely tuned universe-generating process work."

Robin Collins

"The multiverse idea rests on assumptions that would be laughed out of town if they came from a religious text. The theory requires as much suspension of disbelief as any religion. Join the church that believes in the existence of invisible objects fifty billion galaxies wide!"

Journalist Gregg Easterbrook

OPTIONAL DISCUSSION QUESTIONS
for Those Investigating Christianity

• Is it possible that the universe could have been more precisely tuned with a better outcome?

• Physicist Freeman Dyson was quoted in the *New York Times* as saying, "The universe in some sense must have known that we were coming." What do you think he meant by this statement? Does it appear probable or even possible to you that the laws of nature have been carefully arranged so that a Creator could be "discovered"? Or is there another explanation? Elaborate.

• To what degree does the belief in a Creator necessitate a belief that there are no other habitable planets other than earth? In other words, if there is life beyond earth, does this preclude the existence of God? Why or why not?

• Do you think it is necessary to collect hard evidence in order to conclude whether or not something is true? For example, just because we don't have evidence to support the multiple-universe theory doesn't necessarily mean multiple universes don't exist. Do you agree or disagree? Why?

• Robin Collins explains that "though invoking God may not be strictly part of science, it is in the spirit of science to follow the evidence and its implications wherever they lead us." Do you agree that if the facts fit with a "God hypothesis," the field of science should be open to it?

Between Sessions

Personal Reflection

> But ask the animals, and they will teach you,
>   or the birds in the sky, and they will tell you;
> or speak to the earth, and it will teach you,
>   or let the fish of the sea inform you.
> Which of all these does not know
>   that the hand of the LORD has done this?
> In his hand is the life of every creature
>   and the breath of all mankind.
>
> (Job 12:7 – 10)

1. The book of Job is considered to be the oldest book in the Bible, written in a poetic style to convey one man's experience with God. In the above verses, what does Job seem to believe about the Lord? What leads him to this conclusion?

2. The more you learn of the astronomical odds of the incredible razor's-edge precision of the universe, how likely does the existence of a Creator become to you? What do the intricacies of creation reveal about the One who created it all? Describe what the Creator might be like.

3. Is it possible that humankind will someday *know* everything? What are the implications of your answer? Can we ever become equal to the One who "laid the earth's foundation" (Job 38:4)? Will we ever have the power to "[give] orders to the morning, or [show] the dawn its place" (Job 38:12)? What do you believe about our ultimate potential and limitations?

4. In what ways is God speaking to you at this moment through your observations of creation and his words from the Bible? Read Job 38:1–12, 18 and then respond sincerely to him in your own words. Remember that God invites you to talk to him freely and openly! He welcomes your honesty and your doubts. And he just may have some answers for you too, if you're listening.

Personal Reading

Please read the following book content in preparation for session five:

> *The Case for a Creator*, chapter 8: The Evidence of Biochemistry
>
> Or, *The Case for a Creator Student Edition*, chapter 5: Mousetraps and Molecular Machines

The Evidence
of Biochemistry

So far, the evidence from the telescope to the microscope was pointing powerfully in the direction of a Creator — a circumstance I never would have dreamed possible back in my days as a student. I was left with an urgent desire to continue my investigation. Still, I also was experiencing an underlying skepticism. Would the case for a Creator hold up when it was scrutinized more carefully and when I could cross-examine experts with all of the questions that plagued me?

Lee Strobel, *The Case for a Creator*

Watch This!

Video Teaching Segment

Space is provided to take notes on anything that stands out to you.

"We have always underestimated the cell ... The entire cell can be viewed as a factory that contains an elaborate network of interlocking assembly lines, each of which is composed of a set of large protein machines."

— Bruce Alberts, president, National Academy of Sciences

Discuss This!

1. What's your reaction to the fact that a eukaryotic cell, a basic unit of a life, is a complicated molecular machine, a tenth of the size of the head of a pin, made up of about three billion units of DNA?

2. Consider the bacterial flagellum described in the video. Do you agree with Michael Behe that the parts of this machine could not have been assembled by chance? Why or why not?

THINK ABOUT THIS!

"The flagellum's propeller can spin at ten thousand revolutions per minute. As a car aficionado, I was staggered by that statistic! A friend had recently given me a ride in his exotic high-performance sports car, and I knew it wasn't capable of generating that many rpms. Even the notoriously high-revving Honda S2000, with a state-of-the-art, four-cylinder, two-liter, dual-overhead-cam aluminum block engine, featuring four valves per cylinder and variable intake and exhaust valve timing, has a redline of only nine thousand rpms."

Lee Strobel

3. Howard Berg of Harvard has labeled the flagellum "the most efficient machine in the universe." Indeed, biologists agree it's more efficient than any machine humankind has ever produced—especially on its microscopic scale. Do you think we will ever be able to build something more efficient? Why or why not? If that breakthrough were ever to occur, would that impact your assessment of the flagellum?

THINK ABOUT THIS!

"One scientist described a single-cell organism as a high-tech factory, complete with artificial languages and their decoding systems, memory banks for information storage and retrieval, elegant control systems regulating the automated assembly of parts and components, error fail-safe and proof-reading devices utilized for quality control, assembly processes involving the principle of prefabrication and modular construction … and a capacity not equaled in any of our own most advanced machines, for it would be capable of replicating its entire structure within a matter of a few hours."

Franklin M. Harold, *The Way of the Cell*

4. What do you think accounts for the remarkable complexity and apparent design of the microscopic machinery contained within the cell?

"Most scientists speculated that the deeper they delved into the cell, the more simplicity they would find. But the opposite happened."
— Biochemist Michael Behe, Lehigh University

5. Michael Behe claims that Darwinism was a lot more plausible when we were thinking of cells in terms of globs of protoplasm (like gelatin) rather than molecular machines. Do you agree or disagree with Behe's assessment? Explain.

FAST FACT

Biochemistry: *The study of the chemical characteristics and reactions of particular living organisms or biological substances*

Microbiology: *A branch of biology dealing particularly with microscopic forms of life*

Nanotechnology: *The art of manipulating materials on an atomic or molecular scale, especially to build microscopic devices*

6. Read the "Think About This!" box on the next page. How does the irreducibly complex cell potentially pose a problem for Darwin's theory that all living systems have been formed by numerous, successive, slight modifications over time by natural selection? Elaborate.

THINK ABOUT THIS!

"A system or device is irreducibly complex if it has a number of different components that all work together to accomplish the task of the system, and if you were to remove one of the components, the system would no longer function. An irreducibly complex system is highly unlikely to be built piece-by-piece through Darwinian processes, because the system has to be fully present in order for it to function.

"The illustration I like to use is a mousetrap. If you take away any one of the parts — the spring or the holding bar or whatever — then it's not like the mousetrap becomes half as efficient as it used to be or it only catches half as many mice. Instead, it doesn't catch any mice. It's broken. It doesn't work at all."

Michael Behe

"Evolution can't produce an irreducibly complex biological machine suddenly, all at once, because it's much too complicated. The odds against that would be prohibitive. And you can't produce it directly by numerous, successive, slight modifications of a precursor system, because any precursor system would be missing a part and consequently couldn't function. There would be no reason for it to exist. And natural selection chooses systems that are already working."

Michael Behe

"Genetic studies have shown that between thirty and thirty-five proteins are needed to create a functional flagellum. I haven't even begun to describe all of its complexities; we don't even know the roles of all its proteins. But at a minimum you need at least three parts — a paddle, a rotor, and a motor — that are made up of various proteins. Eliminate one of those parts and you don't get a flagellum that only spins at five thousand rpms; you get a flagellum that simply doesn't work at all. So it's irreducibly complex — and a huge stumbling block to Darwinian theory."

Michael Behe

7. Charles Darwin wrote in *The Origin of Species*, "If it could be demonstrated that any complex organ existed which could not possibly have been formed by numerous, successive, slight modifications, my theory would absolutely break down." Does Darwin's theory pass or fail his own test for the evolution of irreducibly complex systems? If Darwin were alive today, do you think he would continue to support his own theory? Why or why not?

OPTIONAL DISCUSSION QUESTIONS
for Those Investigating Christianity

- As scientists peer deeper and deeper into the workings of cells, do you believe they will find more or less complexity? How might this influence your opinion about whether the cell is designed or the product of evolutionary development?

- How do you feel about the idea that your body is basically comprised of millions of microscopic machines? How does this fact change how you view yourself?

- In what ways are we machine-like? What distinguishes humans from machines or animals?

- In the video segment, Michael Behe compares the flagellum to an outboard motor. If a tornado were to blow through a metal factory, what do you think the odds are that an outboard motor could ever get assembled by chance? Is it even possible? Likewise, without the intervention of some kind of intelligence, what are the odds for the chance assemblage of a single flagellum?

- Is Intelligent Design the only way, or one of many ways, to explain the origin of complex systems such as a mousetrap, an outboard motor, or a cell? How might new discoveries of the cell impact your view of a Creator?

Between Sessions

Personal Reflection

> *For you created my inmost being;*
> > *you knit me together in my mother's womb.*
> *I praise you because I am fearfully and wonderfully made;*
> > *your works are wonderful,*
> > *I know that full well.*
> *My frame was not hidden from you*
> > *when I was made in the secret place.*
>
> (Psalm 139:13–15a)

1. What have you discovered in this session that has surprised or impacted you the most? Is it the factory-like complexity of a single cell? The motor-like design of the bacterial flagellum? Or is it the realization that your own body is made up of millions of these microscopic machines?

2. What do you think accounts for the remarkable complexity and design of this microscopic machinery? Is it Darwinian natural selection or is it possible that some kind of intelligent mind was the engineer?

3. According to Psalm 139:13–15a (see the previous page), what does the Bible claim is God's role in the creation of human life? With all you've discovered about the intricacies of the cell, do you have a new level of appreciation for how you've been so ingeniously "knit together"? Would you agree that the human body, even at the microscopic level, has been "fearfully and wonderfully made"?

4. Psalm 139 is a song of praise for the mastermind behind it all—the Lord of all creation! Do you feel humbled or awed as you look more deeply into God's works? What do you think of these words from Francis Collins, the director of the Human Genome Project: "We human scientists have an opportunity to understand the elegance and wisdom of God's creation in a way that is truly exhilarating. When a scientist discovers something that no human knew before, but God did—that is both an occasion for scientific excitement and, for a believer, also an occasion for worship."

5. Do you feel exhilarated or excited by these glimpses into the ingenious mind of the Creator? Read the Psalm passage again. At this point in your spiritual journey, do you feel any sense of awe or even praise for God? If so, why don't you open your heart and speak to him about it at this moment—who knows what else he might reveal to you?

Personal Reading

Please read the following book content in preparation for session six:

> *The Case for a Creator*, chapter 9: The Evidence of Biological Information

> Or, *The Case for a Creator Student Edition*, chapter 6: DNA and the Origin of Life

SESSION 6

DNA and the Origin of Life

Going far back into time, Christians have reached a far different conclusion: Earth was created by God as the stage upon which the human drama would be played out. What's amazing about modern science, including new discoveries just within the last few years, is that this view of the universe seems to be far better supported today than in ancient times ... In hindsight, my materialistic philosophy had been built on a foundation that history has subsequently dismantled piece by piece.

Lee Strobel, *The Case for a Creator*

Watch This!

Video Teaching Segment

Space is provided to take notes on anything that stands out to you.

"Einstein said, 'God does not play dice.'
He was right. God plays Scrabble."
— Philip Gold, Discovery Institute

Discuss This!

1. Where do you think the information contained in DNA comes from? How did it arise in the first place? Can you think of another source, besides intelligence, that is capable of producing information?

THINK ABOUT THIS!

"We know from our experience that we can convey information with a twenty-six-letter alphabet, or twenty-two, or thirty — or even just two characters, like the zeros and ones used in the binary code in computers. One of the most extraordinary discoveries of the twentieth century is that DNA actually stores information — the detailed instructions for assembling proteins — in the form of a four-character digital code. The characters happen to be chemicals called adenine, guanine, cytosine,

cont.

and thymine. Scientists represent them with the letters A, G, C, and T, and that's appropriate because they function as alphabetic characters in the genetic text. Properly arranging those four 'bases' will instruct the cell to build different sequences of amino acids, which are the building blocks of proteins. Different arrangements of characters yield different sequences of amino acids."

Stephen C. Meyer

2. Stephen Meyer asks, "Imagine trying to generate even a simple book by throwing Scrabble letters onto the floor. Or imagine closing your eyes and picking Scrabble letters out of a bag. Are you going to produce *Hamlet* in anything like the time of the known universe?" What do you think? How long would it take to toss Scrabble letters in the air and produce a simple book by chance? How long would it take to produce *Hamlet*? Now, how probable is it that random chance produced the libraries of information contained in DNA? Is this a fair analogy? Why or why not?

THINK ABOUT THIS!

"Human DNA contains more organized information than the Encyclopædia Britannica. *If the full text of the encyclopedia were to arrive in computer code from outer space, most people would regard this as proof of the existence of extraterrestrial intelligence. But when seen in nature, it is explained as the workings of random forces."*

George Sim Johnston, *Did Darwin Get It Right?*

3. Read George Sim Johnston's quote above. Do you agree that most people would attribute code from outer space to extraterrestrial intelligence, and yet at the same time attribute code from nature to random chance? What are some possible explanations for this inconsistency?

THINK ABOUT THIS!

"Based on our uniform and repeated experience (which is the basis of all scientific reasoning about the past), there is only one known cause of information, and that cause is intelligence. Whether we're looking at a hieroglyphic inscription, a section of text in a book, or computer software, if you have information and you trace it back to its source, invariably you come to intelligence. Therefore, when you find information inscribed along the backbone of the DNA molecule in the cell, the most rational inference — based upon repeated experience — is that an intelligence of some kind played a role in the origin of that information.

Stephen C. Meyer

"We've seen that neither chance, nor chance combined with natural selection, nor self-organizational processes have the causal power to produce information. But we do know of one entity that does have the required causal powers to produce information, and that's intelligence. Whenever you find a sequential arrangement that's complex and corresponds to an independent pattern or functional requirement, this kind of information is always the product of intelligence. Scientists in many fields recognize this connection between information and intelligence. When archaeologists discovered the Rosetta Stone, they didn't think its inscriptions were the product of random chance or self-organizational processes. Obviously, the sequential arrangements of symbols was conveying information, and it was a reasonable assumption that intelligence created it. The same principle is true for DNA."

Stephen C. Meyer

5. Read Stephen Meyer's quotes above and on the previous page. If you were a teacher evaluating Meyer on how well he defended his thesis that DNA is best explained by an intelligent cause, what grade would you give him? What reasons would you give in defending that grade?

"DNA is like a software program, only much more complex than anything we've ever devised."
— Bill Gates, founder of Microsoft

5. After considering and discussing the most recent scientific evidence in these sessions, do you think it is logical and rational, or illogical and irrational, to conclude that there is something divine behind creation? Elaborate.

"An honest man, armed with all the knowledge available to us now, could only state that in some sense, the origin of life appears at the moment to be almost a miracle, so many are the conditions which would have had to have been satisfied to get it going."
— Nobel Prize winner Francis Crick

THINK ABOUT THIS!

"When we look at the evidence from cosmology, physics, biology, and human consciousness, we find that theism has amazing explanatory scope and power. The existence of God explains this broad range of evidence more simply, adequately, and comprehensively than any other worldview, including its main competitors: naturalism or pantheism. And the discovery of corroborating or supportive evidence is accelerating."

Stephen C. Meyer

"One of the most interesting things I've learned as I've gone on this journey of scientific discovery has been that you don't have to commit intellectual suicide to acknowledge the existence of an Intelligent Designer, because today science is pointing more directly toward a Creator than at any time in the history of the world."

Lee Strobel

6. What can science tell us about the nature of a Creator—his qualities, his attributes, his priorities? What *can't* it tell us? What are some other ways a Creator might make himself known? What are other reliable sources of information that could be pursued in investigating God?

"I cannot imagine how the clockwork of the universe can exist without a clockmaker."
                                    — Voltaire

THINK ABOUT THIS!

"The best data we have [concerning the origin of the universe] are exactly what I would have predicted, had I nothing to go on but the five books of Moses, the Psalms, and the Bible as a whole."

Nobel Prize – winning physicist Arno Penzias

"Ironically, the picture of the universe bequeathed to us by the most advanced twentieth-century science is closer in spirit to the vision presented in ... Genesis than anything offered by science since Copernicus."

Atheist-turned-Christian Patrick Glynn, in *God: The Evidence*

"The exquisite order displayed by our scientific understanding of the physical world calls for the divine."

Vera Kistiakowsky, professor emeritus of physics,
Massachusetts Institute of Technology

"People see God every day, they just don't recognize him."

Pearl Bailey

"It is only through the supernatural that I can understand the mystery of existence."

Cosmologist Allan Sandage

"From a knowledge of God's work we shall know him."

Robert Boyle, father of modern chemistry

OPTIONAL DISCUSSION QUESTIONS
for Those Investigating Christianity

- To what extent does it appear that the laws of nature have been carefully arranged so that they can be discovered? Does this matter? Why or why not? What might be the significance behind this "discoverability factor"?

- Lee Strobel believes the implications of the scientific evidence are profound. He wonders if the information inside every cell in every living creature could be the signature of a Creator. What do you think? Is God's fingerprint or signature on every living thing? Do agree with Lee's assessment? Why or why not?

- Physicist Paul Davies concludes that the universe has been put together with astonishing ingenuity. Do you agree with Davies's conclusion? Why or why not? What about things like black holes that gobble up other celestial bodies? Why would something like this have been designed?

- If the evidence of science points toward a Creator, then where does faith fit in? In other words, what's the interplay between facts and faith?

- If you are convinced that a Creator does exist, to what extent do you think it's possible to have a personal relationship with him? To what degree do you want to know and experience God? What might this relational experience be like for you?

In the Coming Days

Personal Reflection

> *The heavens declare the glory of God;*
> *the skies proclaim the work of his hands.*
> *Day after day they pour forth speech;*
> *night after night they reveal knowledge.*
> *They have no speech, they use no words;*
> *no sound is heard from them.*
> *Yet their voice goes out into all the earth,*
> *their words to the ends of the world.*
>
> (Psalm 19:1–4a)

1. What is your immediate reaction to the above Bible verses? What do you think the ancient author of this psalm was trying to express? What is meant by the words, "Day after day they pour forth speech; night after night they reveal knowledge"? Do you agree that the heavens declare the handiwork of a Creator, that this kind of "speech" supercedes cultural and language barriers?

2. Is the author of the psalm indifferent to the expanse of the universe or is he awed by it? Can you relate to his sentiments about the world around you in any way? How do *you* feel when you look into the night sky on a clear evening and see a pattern of distant suns or the full, round moon hanging low and large on the horizon?

3. Has your sense of wonder been in any way reinvigorated by your study and discussion of *The Case for a Creator*? If so, what has impacted you most? Is it the scientific community's doubts about Darwinism? The evidence that the universe had a finite beginning just as the Bible has always stated all along? The incredible fine-tuning and razor's edge precision within which all life hangs in the balance? The intricate and irreducibly complex nature of a simple cell? Or the discovery of the vast libraries of information stored in DNA—the complicated language of life? Has your belief system been in any way challenged as you've read, listened, questioned, and discussed the most recent scientific discoveries that show how improbable and miraculous life really is?

4. Romans 1:20 says, "For since the creation of the world God's invisible qualities — his eternal power and divine nature — have been clearly seen, being understood from what has been made, so that people are without excuse." In what ways have you seen the fingerprints of God at work in creation? How has your opinion changed recently? How much more evidence of God's invisible qualities do we have today than the author of Romans had?

5. If you're willing, take some time now to talk to the God who created and sustains it all. If you feel ready — and haven't done so already — you could even invite this great and powerful God into your life. Start by praying something like, "I don't know very much about you, but I believe you're real and you're powerful, and you can do anything. Please come into my life and teach me. Forgive me for ignoring you in any way and help me to know you more." If you pray a prayer like this with sincerity, the God of the Bible promises he will answer you.

Small Group Leader Helps

To ensure a successful small group experience, read the following information before beginning.

Group Preparation

Whether your small group has been meeting together for years or is gathering for the first time, be sure to designate a consistent time and place to work through the six sessions. Once you establish the when and where of your times together, select a facilitator who will keep discussions on track and an eye on the clock. If you choose to rotate this responsibility, assign the six sessions to their respective facilitators up front, so that group members can prepare their thoughts and questions prior to the session they are responsible for leading. Follow the same assignment procedure should your group want to serve any snacks or beverages.

A Note to Facilitators

As facilitator, you are responsible for honoring the agreed-upon time frame of each meeting, for prompting helpful discussion among your group, and for keeping the dialogue equitable by drawing out quieter members and helping more talkative members to remember that others' insights are valued in your group.

You might find it helpful to preview each session's video teaching segment and then scan the discussion questions that pertain to it, highlighting various questions that you want to be sure to cover during your group's meeting. Ask God in advance of your time together to guide your group's discussion, and then be sensitive to the direction he wishes to lead.

Urge participants to bring their study guide, pen, and a Bible to every gathering. Encourage them to consider buying a copy of *The Case for a Creator* book by Lee Strobel to supplement this study.

Session Format

Each session of the study guide includes the following group components:

- **Watch This!** — Space is provided for individual notes and insights as the group views the session's video presentation, about 30 minutes.

- **Discuss This!** — Video-related and Bible exploration questions reinforce the session content and elicit personal input from every group member. The boxed content ("Think About This!" and "Fast Fact") interspersed throughout this section bears directly on surrounding questions. Either have group members read this content to themselves, read it aloud yourself, or have group members take turns reading it aloud. The latter two options will take longer.

- **Optional Discussion Questions for Those Investigating Christianity** — At the end of the main discussion section are further questions for groups that have more time or interest. You may even choose to substitute a question or two for questions in the main discussion section.

Additionally, in each session you will find a **Between Sessions** section (**In the Coming Days** after session six) that includes suggestions for personal reflection and response as well as recommended reading from *The Case for a Creator* book in preparation for the next session.

The Case for a Creator

A Journalist Investigates Scientific Evidence That Points toward God

Lee Strobel
New York Times *Bestselling Author*

"My road to atheism was paved by science . . . But, ironically, so was my later journey to God." – **Lee Strobel**

During his academic years, Lee Strobel became convinced that God was outmoded, a belief that colored his ensuing career as an award-winning journalist at the *Chicago Tribune*. Science had made the idea of a Creator irrelevant — or so Strobel thought.

But today science is pointing in a different direction. In recent years, a diverse and impressive body of research has increasingly supported the conclusion that the universe was intelligently designed. At the same time, Darwinism has faltered in the face of concrete facts and hard reason.

Has science discovered God? At the very least, it's giving faith an immense boost as new findings emerge about the incredible complexity of our universe. Join Strobel as he reexamines the theories that once led him away from God. Through his compelling and highly readable account, you'll encounter the mind-stretching discoveries from cosmology, cellular biology, DNA research, astronomy, physics, and human consciousness that present astonishing evidence in *The Case for a Creator*.

Available in stores and online!

The Case for Christ: A DVD Study

Investigating the Evidence for Jesus

Lee Strobel and Garry Poole

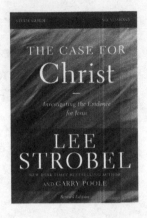

Is there credible evidence that Jesus of Nazareth really is the Son of God?

Skeptics dismiss the Jesus of the Gospels by claiming there is no evidence in the case for Christ. Lee Strobel disagrees. The former legal journalist and one-time atheist knows how to ask tough questions. His own search for truth about Jesus led him to faith in Christ.

Now Strobel invites you and your group to investigate the truth about Jesus Christ leading to the facts that guided Strobel from atheism to faith in Christ. In this revised six-session video with separate study guide, participants will journey along with Strobel on a quest for the truth about Jesus. Rejecting easy answers, you will sift through fascinating historical evidence as you weigh compelling expert testimony. In the end, groups may very well see Jesus in a new way—and even, like Strobel, find their lives transformed.

The six sessions include:
- The Investigation of a Lifetime
- Eyewitness Evidence
- Evidence Outside the Bible
- Analyzing Jesus
- Evidence for the Resurrection
- Reaching Your Verdict

The Case for Faith: A DVD Study

Investigating the Toughest Objections to Christianity

Lee Strobel and Garry Poole

Does believing in Christ mean refusing to ask hard questions in the midst of doubt?

Doubt is familiar territory for Lee Strobel, the former atheist and award-winning author of books for skeptics and Christians. But he believes that faith and reason go hand in hand, and that Christianity is a defensible religion.

In this six-session revised small group video Bible study, Strobel explores the most common emotional obstacles to faith in Christ. These include the natural inclination to wrestle with faith and doubt, the troubling presence of evil and suffering in the world, and the exclusivity of the Christian gospel. They also include this compelling question: *Can I doubt and be a Christian?*

Through compelling personal stories and experts testimony combined with reflection and interaction, Christians and spiritual seekers will learn how to overcome these obstacles, deepen their spiritual convictions, and find new confidence that Christianity is a reasonable faith.

Sessions include:
- The Challenge of Faith
- Dealing with Doubt
- Evil and Suffering, Part 1
- Evil and Suffering, Part 2
- Why Is Jesus the Only Way to God?
- The Power of Faith

Available in stores and online!

The Case for Christ for Kids Curriculum

Investigating the Truth about Jesus

Lee Strobel with Christopher D. Hudson

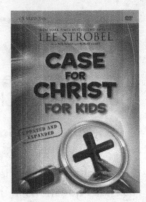

How would the kids in your children's ministry answer friends who ask questions like: Was Jesus really born in a stable? Did his friends tell the truth? Did he really come back from the dead?

In these six lessons children will learn answers to these and other pressing questions in kid-friendly language that will help them grow in their faith. Packed full of well-researched, reliable, and fun investigations of some of the biggest questions kids have, *The Case for Christ for Kids Curriculum* brings Jesus to life by addressing the existence, miracles, ministry, and resurrection of Christ.

This DVD-ROM makes your children's ministry planning simple and includes everything you need for a successful Sunday school, children's church, or VBS program:

- A checklist to help leaders organize each week's study
- Lesson Plans
- Family Pages
- Promotional materials
- AND a VBS expansion kit to help leaders teach *The Case for Christ for Kids Curriculum* as a Vacation Bible School or Backyard Bible Club program

The six sessions include:

- The Case of the Promised Baby
- The Case of the Voice from Heaven
- The Case of the Eyewitnesses
- The Case of the Wedding Crisis
- The Case of the Living Water
- The Case of the Risen Jesus

Available in stores and online!

ZONDERVAN®
.com

Faith Under Fire:
A DVD Study

Exploring Christianity's Ten Toughest Questions

Lee Strobel and Garry Poole

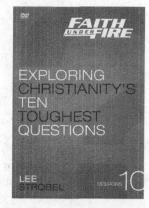

Faith Under Fire is a ten-session small group Bible study exploring Christianity's toughest questions, including the existence of God, Christianity and Islam, the reliability of the Bible, and faith and science. On the video, bestselling author Lee Strobel hosts spirited discussions between well-respected Christians, people of other faiths, and people with no faith at all, on the some of the most important spiritual and social issues of our time. The participant's guide will help you and your group sift through and gain understanding on these controversial and relevant issues that surround the Christian faith and many of its most pertinent cultural issues. Strobel provides additional comments to guide small group discussion.

Sessions include:
1. Is the Supernatural Real?
2. Is Jesus a Prophet or the Son of God?
3. Did Jesus Rise from the Dead?
4. Do All Roads Lead to God?
5. Is the Bible Bogus?
6. Does Science Point to a Creator?
7. Is Anything Beyond Forgiveness?
8. Why Does God Allow Pain and Suffering?
9. The Mystery of the Trinity?
10. Do Christians and Muslims Worship the Same God?

Available in stores and online!

Share Your Thoughts

With the Author: Your comments will be forwarded to the author when you send them to *zauthor@zondervan.com*.

With Zondervan: Submit your review of this book by writing to *zreview@zondervan.com*.

Free Online Resources at
www.zondervan.com

Daily Bible Verses and Devotions: Enrich your life with daily Bible verses or devotions that help you start every morning focused on God. Visit www.zondervan.com/newsletters.

Free Email Publications: Sign up for newsletters on Christian living, academic resources, church ministry, fiction, children's resources, and more. Visit www.zondervan.com/newsletters.

Zondervan Bible Search: Find and compare Bible passages in a variety of translations at www.zondervanbiblesearch.com.

Other Benefits: Register to receive online benefits like coupons and special offers, or to participate in research.